HOW TO SPENDING MONEY IMPULSIVELY

How I stopped Impulsive spending Habits, Paid off my debts, Saved more and now Live my Financial Dreams

Elisha R. Ackman

All rights reserved. No part of this publication may be reproduced, distributed, or transmitted in any form or by any means, including photocopying, recording, or other electronic or mechanical methods, without the prior written permission of the publisher, except in the case of brief quotations embodied in critical reviews and certain other noncommercial uses permitted by copyright law.

Copyright © Elisha R. Ackman, 2024.

Table of Contents

Introduction 5
Chapter 1: Understanding Impulsive Spending 11
    The Psychology Behind Impulsive Spending. 11
    Recognizing Your Spending Triggers 13
    The Impact of Impulsive Spending on Financial Health... 14
Chapter 2: The Debt Trap 17
    How Impulsive Spending Leads to Debt 17
    The Real Cost of Debt................................... 18
    Stories of Debt: Personal Experiences 20
    The Impact of Impulsive Spending on Financial Health... 21
Chapter 3: Dreaming Financially 23
    Defining Your Financial Dreams 23
    The Importance of Setting Realistic Financial Goals 24
    Vision Versus Reality: Where You Stand........ 25
Chapter 4: Mindful Spending 27
    The Concept of Mindful Spending 27
    Techniques for Mindful Spending 28
    From Mindless to Mindful: My Journey 30
Chapter 5: Creating a Budget That Works 33
    The Basics of Effective Budgeting 33
    Customizing Your Budget: Ubong's Method .. 34
    Sticking to Your Budget: Strategies for Success 36
Chapter 6: Debt Reduction Strategies 41

Assessing and Prioritizing Your Debts............ 41
Methods for Paying Down Debt..................... 42
My Debt-Free Journey: A Case Study 44

Chapter 7: Building Healthy Financial Habits . 47
Identifying and Changing Bad Financial Habits... 47
The Power of Consistency............................. 49
Habit Formation Techniques for Financial Success 50

Chapter 8: Investing in Your Future................ 55
Understanding Basic Investments 55
Making Smart Investment Choices 56
Risk Management: Learning from My Mistakes... 58

Chapter 9: Maintaining Financial Discipline.... 63
Overcoming Temptations and Setbacks 63
Long-term Financial Discipline: My Personal Strategies... 65
Celebrating Financial Milestones 67

Chapter 10: Living Your Financial Dream 71
What Living Your Financial Dream Really Means 71
Real-Life Stories of Financial Success 72
Preparing for the Future: My Final Thoughts . 74

30-day Practical Action Plan 79
Week 1: Assessment and Planning 79
Week 2: Building Better Habits 81
Week 3: Debt Reduction Focus 83
Week 4: Solidifying Financial Discipline.......... 84

Introduction

Not too long ago, my financial life was a mess. I was the king of impulsive spending, and debt was my loyal subject. Every day, I'd find new things to buy - a cool gadget, trendy clothes, or just something to lift my spirits. It felt good at the moment, but it was a fleeting happiness. As soon as I got home, the excitement would vanish, leaving me with nothing but regret and a pile of unopened bills.

I remember sitting in my small apartment one night, surrounded by all these things I had bought. It hit me hard. I was drowning in debt, and all these purchases, which I thought would make me happy, were actually doing the opposite. I was trapped in a cycle of spending and owing, and it was suffocating me. The worst part? I couldn't see a way out.

But then, something inside me clicked. I realized that if I didn't take control of my finances, nobody else would. It was time to face the music. I started by simply writing down everything I owed. It was scary to see the total amount of my debt, but it was also a wake-up call. From that day, I made a promise to myself: no more running, no more hiding. It was time to tackle my financial problems head-on.

The journey wasn't easy. I had to change a lot of my habits. I cut down on eating out, started making coffee at home instead of buying it every day, and learned to differentiate between what I needed and what I wanted. Every time I resisted an impulsive buy, I felt a little stronger, a little more in control.

Paying off my debts was a slow process, but with each payment, I felt lighter. I remember the day I paid off my first credit card. It was a small victory, but it meant the world to me. It was proof that I could do this, that I could be the master of my finances.

As I continued to pay off my debts, I started learning about saving and investing. I was no expert, but I was determined to secure a better financial future for myself. I began setting aside a little money each month, no matter how tight things were. It wasn't just about saving money; it was about investing in my future.

Today, I'm living a life I never thought possible. I'm debt-free, and I've built a safety net that gives me peace of mind. I don't worry about money like I used to. I've learned the true value of money, and more importantly, I've learned to respect it.

I'm sharing my story with you because I know there are many out there who are where I was – feeling trapped and hopeless under the weight of debt and impulsive spending. I want you to know that it's possible to turn things around. It takes patience, discipline, and a willingness to change, but trust me, it's worth it.

In this book, I'll take you through the steps I took to regain control of my finances. These aren't just theories; they're real strategies that worked for me. I hope my story inspires you to take that first step towards financial freedom. Remember, it's never too late to rewrite your financial story. Let's do this together!

Chapter 1: Understanding Impulsive Spending

The Psychology Behind Impulsive Spending

Have you ever walked into a store, planning to buy just one thing, but walked out with a bag full of items you hadn't planned on buying? That's impulsive spending. It's when you make unplanned purchases, often driven by emotions rather than need or careful thought.

But why do we do it? Often, it's about seeking a quick mood boost. For me, buying something new always gave me a rush, a fleeting moment of excitement. It's similar to craving a sweet treat when we're feeling down; it provides instant gratification. This behavior is linked to the reward center in our brain. When we buy something on impulse, our brain releases dopamine, a feel-good neurotransmitter, making us momentarily happy.

But there's more to it. Sometimes, we spend impulsively because of social influences or marketing tricks. How many times have you bought something just because it was on sale, or because everyone else was buying it? Retailers know this psychology and use tactics like limited-time offers or displaying items at the checkout line to tempt us.

Recognizing Your Spending Triggers

Identifying what triggers your impulsive spending is crucial. For me, it was often boredom or stress. Whenever I felt low or anxious, I found myself wandering into shops or browsing online stores. For others, it might be peer pressure or the thrill of a sale.

Start by tracking your spending habits. Keep a small notebook or use an app to jot down every purchase you make. Note down how you were feeling or what was happening around you when you made these purchases. You'll begin to see patterns. Maybe you're more likely to buy something unplanned when you're out with certain friends, or when you're feeling down after a hard day at work.

Recognizing these triggers is the first step to gaining control. Once you know what prompts your impulsive buys, you can start to develop strategies to combat them. For instance, if stress leads you to shop, try finding healthier ways to cope, like going for a walk or practising meditation.

The Impact of Impulsive Spending on Financial Health

Impulsive spending might seem harmless at the moment, especially if the items are inexpensive. But over time, these purchases add up and can significantly impact your financial health. I learned this the hard way. At first, I didn't think my occasional splurges were a big deal. But when I sat down and looked at my credit card statements, I was shocked. All those little purchases had accumulated into a mountain of debt. Not only was I spending more than I was earning, but I was also paying interest on my credit card balances, which just made things worse.

Impulsive spending can derail your budget, savings, and financial goals. It can lead to a cycle of debt, as it did in my case. When you're constantly playing catch-up with your finances, it's hard to save for important goals like buying a house, planning for retirement, or even just having a safety net for emergencies.

Moreover, the stress of financial trouble can affect other areas of your life, including your mental and physical health. The constant worry about money was affecting my sleep, my mood, and my relationships. It was a wake-up call for me. I realized I needed to change not just for the sake of my wallet, but for my overall well-being.

Understanding impulsive spending involves recognizing the psychological factors that drive it, identifying your personal spending triggers, and acknowledging the impact it has on your financial health. For me, the journey to overcoming impulsive spending started with these realizations. It wasn't easy, but by understanding the why and how of my spending habits, I was able to take control, make better choices, and start working towards a healthier financial future.

Chapter 2: The Debt Trap

How Impulsive Spending Leads to Debt

Impulsive spending may sometimes seem like a harmless habit, particularly when it's only a few bucks here and there. But, as I found, these modest costs soon mount up, sending many into a hole of debt. It's like filling a bucket with a gradual trickle; you don't notice it's full until it begins to overflow.

For me, the pattern seemed modest at first. I'd see something I desired, and without much consideration, I'd purchase it, generally with my credit card. The issue with credit cards is that they create a feeling of disconnection from actual money; it's simply a fast swipe or a touch. Before I knew it, I was only making minimum payments on my cards, and the interest rates were blowing the total amount due.

This pattern of hasty shopping and paying just the minimum on credit cards is a frequent way individuals go into debt. It's like being in quicksand; the more you battle without a strategy, the deeper you fall.

The Real Cost of Debt

Debt isn't simply about the money you owe. It comes with a cost that extends beyond money and cents. For starters, there's the interest. When you maintain a debt on your credit card, you're not just paying back what you borrowed; you're also paying interest, which may be rather substantial. This implies that a $50 shirt might wind up costing you $70 or $80 over time if you're not cautious.

But the penalty of debt isn't merely financial. It takes a toll on your mental and emotional well-being. I recall evenings laying awake, concerned about how I was going to pay off my increasing obligations. It was a continual source of stress, impacting my mood, my career, and even my relationships.

Furthermore, being in debt restricts your financial independence. Your possibilities for the future become constricted. Whether it's saving for a home, planning a trip, or simply having the security of an emergency fund, debt may put your ambitions on hold.

Stories of Debt: Personal Experiences

I recall meeting a young couple, Sarah and Tom, at a financial wellness lecture. Like me, they had slipped into the financial trap via hasty spending. Luxurious trips, the newest technologies, and eating out had become a regular part of their lives. They didn't grasp the amount of their debt until they wanted to purchase a house and were refused a mortgage.

Their tale is a typical illustration of how simple it is to slip into debt and how hard it can be to climb out. They had to dramatically adjust their lifestyle, cutting out any needless purchases and dedicating most of their money to pay off debt. It was a rough road, but they emerged stronger, with great lessons learnt.

The Impact of Impulsive Spending on Financial Health

Linking back to my personal life, the effect of impulsive spending on my financial health was a painful fact to confront. Each impulsive purchase appeared little in isolation, but combined, they caused a substantial hole in my budget.

The first step in resolving this was admitting the issue. I had to accept that my spending habits were unsustainable and were damaging my financial future. Once I accomplished that, I could start making modifications.

The route to financial health involves setting and keeping to a budget, differentiating desires from necessities, and finding healthy methods to cope with emotions rather than via buying. It was also about learning to accept and cherish what I already had, rather than continuously wanting something new.

Recovering from the consequences of impulsive spending is a struggle. It entails altering behaviors, gaining financial discipline, and occasionally, making sacrifices. But the peace of mind and financial security that come with it are worth every effort.

Chapter 3: Dreaming Financially

Defining Your Financial Dreams

When I speak about financial aspirations, it's not simply about desiring more money. It's about what that money can do for you — the independence, the security, and the chances it can give. For each individual, these dreams could appear different. Maybe it's purchasing a house, touring the globe, or having the peace of mind that comes with a good retirement plan.

For me, my financial ideal was to be debt-free and have enough cash to not worry about emergencies. But it's not enough to merely have a faint concept of your ideal. You need to describe it clearly. What precisely do you aim to accomplish financially? Is it paying off all your bills, saving a set amount of money, or something else? Be as precise as possible. This clarity will be your guiding light as you move towards your objectives.

The Importance of Setting Realistic Financial Goals

I learnt the hard way that establishing unreasonable objectives may lead to frustration and failures. In my early days of financial planning, I had grandiose goals to pay off all my debt in a year. But this was far from feasible given my salary and costs. When I failed to fulfil these unreasonable expectations, it led to disillusionment and demotivation.

The idea is to create manageable, realistic objectives. Start small. If you're in debt, maybe your first aim is to pay off the lowest bill. Then, go on to the next one. If you're saving, start by putting away a tiny amount each month. It might be as low as $50. What's crucial is that you're taking a step forward.

Remember, your financial path is a marathon, not a sprint. It's about making continuous, sustained development, not racing towards an unachievable finish line.

Vision Versus Reality: Where You Stand

Dreaming is necessary, but it must be based in reality. This entails taking a critical, honest look at where you now are financially. For me, this was a challenging but essential step. I had to sit down and compute all my debts, analyze my monthly income, and watch my expenditures. It was unsettling to see the figures, but it was also inspiring.

To acquire a comprehensive view of your financial condition, start by listing your debts, income, and spending. This will provide you a comprehensive sense of your financial health. Are you spending more than you earn? Are your loans a substantial chunk of your income? Knowing where you stand is vital in deciding how to get to where you want to be.

Once you have this clarity, you can start bridging the gap between your vision and reality. This entails developing a plan — a budget, a debt payback plan, a savings strategy – and adhering to it. It also includes being prepared to change your strategy as required. Life is unpredictable, and your financial strategy should be flexible enough to accept adjustments.

Chapter 4: Mindful Spending

The Concept of Mindful Spending

Mindful spending is about making financial choices with purpose and mindfulness. It's not just about spending less, but spending smarter — connecting your spending with your beliefs and ambitions. The notion of mindful spending was a game changer for me. It transformed my attitude from just attempting to control impulsive spending to making informed decisions about how I utilized my money.

To understand mindful spending, think of it as the reverse of impulsive spending. Instead of purchasing items on a whim, you stop, ponder, and evaluate whether that purchase genuinely adds value to your life.

It's about questioning oneself, "Do I really need this? Will it help me get towards my financial goals? Does that match with what's essential to me?"

Techniques for Mindful Spending

Adopting mindful spending habits isn't about deprivation. It's about making deliberate decisions. Here are some strategies I found helpful:

1. Track Your Spending: Start by understanding where your money goes. Use a notepad or an app to record every purchase. This exercise alone may be eye-opening.

2. Wait Before You Buy: Impulse buys typically happen in the heat of the moment.

If you find something you desire, wait for a day or two before buying. This cooling-off phase might help you evaluate whether it's a necessity or merely a fleeting desire.

3. Set Spending Priorities: Identify what's genuinely essential to you and manage your money appropriately. For me, experiences like travelling were more significant than possessing the newest electronics.

4. Use Cash Instead of Cards: Paying with cash might make you more mindful of spending. It's a concrete method to see how much you're leaving with, unlike the abstract nature of swiping a card.

5. Reflect on Purchases: Regularly analyze your purchases. Ask yourself whether each purchase was worth it and what you might have done better.

From Mindless to Mindful: My Journey

My path from thoughtless to mindful spending wasn't an overnight shift. It took a lot of trial and error, and a deep dive into my spending patterns and views towards money.

I recall a specific experience that was a turning moment for me. I had hastily purchased a costly watch, enticed by its colorful marketing and a sensation of wanting to reward myself. But the delight was short-lived. Soon after, I had a financial difficulty and found myself regretting the purchase — the money might have been utilized far more wisely.

This encounter pushed me to introspect and finally embrace mindful spending. I began by recording every dime I spent, which was an eye-opener. I witnessed how modest, impulsive purchases piled up to big sums. Then, I adopted the habit of waiting 24 to 48 hours before making any non-essential purchases. Many times, the want to purchase went away.

I also re-evaluated my priorities. I discovered I preferred experiences above stuff, so I began spending more for travel and less for tangible possessions. Paying with cash was another method that made a major impact. It made purchasing seem more genuine and helped reduce impulsive buys.

Reflecting on my purchases, both good and poor, became a practice. Each reflection was a chance to learn and make better decisions next time.

Chapter 5: Creating a Budget That Works

The Basics of Effective Budgeting

Budgeting is the cornerstone of smart financial management, yet it's frequently misunderstood. A budget isn't a financial straitjacket that limits your spending; it's a tool to help you spend intelligently. The first step in efficient budgeting is analyzing your income and spending. Track every dollar you make and spend. This will offer you a clear picture of where your money is going.

Next, classify your costs into requirements (such rent, utilities, food) and desires (like eating out, entertainment). This difference is significant. Needs are basics you can't live without, while desires are good to have. Effective budgeting ensures your requirements are always met and finds a balance for your desires.

Then, define targets for your spending and savings. These should be practical and matched with your financial aspirations. If you're looking to save for a down payment on a home, for instance, your budget should reflect that objective with a distinct savings area.

Customizing Your Budget: Ubong' Method

When I initially began budgeting, I learned that one-size-fits-all tactics didn't work for me. I had to build a method that matched my individual financial condition and ambitions. I titled it "Ubong's Method."

The first stage in my technique was prioritizing my spending. I began with my requirements and ensured they were met. Then, I looked at my desires and asked myself which of them offered me the most pleasure and were worth retaining. For example, I valued dining out with friends more than having a premium TV package. So, I budgeted extra for eating out and cut down on my TV subscription.

The second step was establishing a 'flex category' in my budget. This was a tiny, defined amount of money each month that I could spend on whatever I wanted without feeling bad. It provided me the opportunity to indulge periodically without derailing my budget.

Lastly, I tied my budget to my financial objectives. Every dollar I saved from cutting down on needless costs was channeled towards my objectives, like paying off debt or creating an emergency fund.

Sticking to Your Budget: Strategies for Success

Creating a budget is one thing; adhering to it is another. Here are some ideas that helped me keep on track:

1. Regular Check-ins: I take aside time each week to evaluate my budget and monitor my expenditures. This lets me notice any overspending early and react appropriately.

2. Use Budgeting Tools: There are various applications and tools available that help ease budgeting. I used a basic spreadsheet at first, but eventually upgraded to a budgeting tool that connected to my bank accounts for real-time monitoring.

3. Reward Yourself: It's crucial to recognize modest achievements. When I kept inside my budget for a month, I would reward myself - generally something little but delightful, like a movie night.

4. Be Flexible: Life is unpredictable, and sometimes you need to adapt your budget. If an unexpected expenditure comes up, evaluate where you can cut down in other areas to compensate.

5. Seek Support: Share your financial objectives with a friend or family member. Having someone to share your financial path with may be inspiring and give accountability.

One noteworthy incident of keeping to my budget happened over the Christmas season, generally a period of significant spending for me. That year, I established a tight budget for presents and celebrations. It took inventiveness and some painful decisions – like choosing for homemade presents over store-bought ones – but it was tremendously wonderful to start the new year without the typical financial hangover.

This chapter breaks down the process of efficient budgeting and provides "Ubong's Method," a tailored method to budget management. The chapter highlights the significance of managing your money, prioritizing costs, and creating realistic objectives. It also gives practical ways for keeping to your budget and includes personal experiences to exemplify these themes. This chapter is aimed to encourage readers to establish and manage a budget that matches with their financial ambitions and lifestyle, changing budgeting from a drudgery into a joyful, goal-oriented activity.

Chapter 6: Debt Reduction Strategies

Assessing and Prioritizing Your Debts

Debt might seem like a heavy weight, but with the correct plan, it's possible to lighten it. The first stage in any debt reduction strategy is to examine and prioritize your bills. Make a list of all your bills, including credit card balances, loans, and any other money you owe. Note down the interest rates and minimum payments for each. This will provide you a comprehensive view of your debt status.

Prioritizing debts is key. Generally, it's better to pay off high-interest bills first, since they cost you the most over time. However, other individuals prefer the *'snowball technique,'* where you start by paying off the smallest debt first for a psychological boost, then progress to the next lowest, and so on.

Methods for Paying Down Debt

There are various efficient approaches to combat debt. The way you use relies on your own circumstances and preferences:

1. Obligation Avalanche Method: This entails paying the minimum on all your bills, then using any excess money to pay off the obligation with the highest interest rate. This strategy can save you the most interest over time.

2. Debt Snowball Method: Here, you concentrate on paying off the lowest debt first while paying the minimum on others. Once the lowest debt is paid off, you go to the next smallest. This strategy might deliver rapid victories, keeping you motivated.

3. Consolidation Loans: Sometimes, merging various loans into a single loan with a reduced interest rate may make payments more reasonable.

4. Negotiating with Creditors: In certain circumstances, creditors may be ready to negotiate a settlement or more favorable terms.

My Debt-Free Journey: A Case Study

My road to become debt-free was tough but incredibly satisfying. Initially, the amount of debt I had seemed overwhelming. I had many credit cards with significant amounts and a personal loan. The first thing I did was sit down and list all my loans, from the highest interest rate to the lowest. I was astonished to learn the overall amount I owed, but it was a necessary wake-up call.

I opted to employ the debt avalanche strategy. I maintained making minimal payments on all my obligations but placed whatever additional money I had towards the one with the highest interest rate. This wasn't simple; it needed rigorous planning and cutting down on numerous non-essential spending. But watching the interest on my largest loan reduce each month was very encouraging.

One of the most major adjustments I made was in my attitude to spending. I began to utilizing cash for most purchases, which dramatically controlled my compulsive spending tendencies. I also launched a side job to bring in additional revenue, which went straight towards my debt.

There were difficulties, of course. Unexpected costs came up, and there were months when I couldn't pay as much towards my debt as I planned. But I didn't let it discourage me. I modified my budget, remained focused on my objective, and continued moving ahead.

After many years of devotion and hard work, I made my last loan payment. The joy of being debt-free was indescribable. Not only had I eliminated my obligations, but I had also learnt vital financial discipline and a fresh perspective on money.

This chapter gives a thorough guidance on analyzing and prioritizing debts and discusses practical strategies for paying them down. The chapter also includes my own narrative, presenting a real-life case study of how I handled my debt utilizing these tactics. This chapter attempts to provide readers practical skills and encouragement to go on their own road to being debt-free, highlighting the value of tenacity, discipline, and adaptation in conquering financial issues.

Chapter 7: Building Healthy Financial Habits

Identifying and Changing Bad Financial Habits

Breaking away from unhealthy financial habits is the first step towards a better financial future. It begins with recognizing these tendencies. Common ones include impulsive spending, not monitoring costs, and using credit cards unwisely. For me, impulsive internet purchasing was a huge concern. I regularly purchased goods I didn't need, enticed by offers and discounts.

Changing these patterns needs self-awareness and a willingness to change. Here's how I accomplished it:

1. Track Spending: I began by recording every dime I spent. This eye-opening practice let me realize where my money was going and which items were genuinely important.

2. Created Spending Limits: I created a budget for discretionary spending and adhered to it, no matter what.

3. Avoid Temptations: Unsubscribing from marketing emails and avoiding online buying sites helped limit my impulsive purchases.

Remember, change doesn't happen overnight. Be patient with yourself and acknowledge minor triumphs along the road.

The Power of Consistency

Consistency is crucial to creating and sustaining sound financial habits. It's about making the proper financial choices day after day, not just once in a while. This includes continuously keeping to your budget, routinely analyzing your financial objectives, and continually searching for ways to improve.

I discovered the virtue of consistency the hard way. There were months when I kept closely to my budget, followed by times of relapse into old spending habits. These volatility harmed my financial success. Once I discovered that regular efforts, no matter how tiny, contribute to big outcomes over time, my financial health began improving consistently.

Developing consistency entails developing routines. For instance, I made it a practice to evaluate my budget and financial objectives every Sunday evening. This regimen kept my financial goals fresh in my mind and helped me start each week on the right foot.

Habit Formation Techniques for Financial Success

Building new habits, particularly financial ones, may be tough. However, there are various approaches that might help this process:

1. Start little: Begin with little, doable adjustments. If saving 20% of your salary sounds onerous, start with 5% and gradually raise it.

2. Use Reminders: In the early stages, reminders may be effective. I used to set alarms on my phone for bill payments and weekly budget reviews.

3. Associate New Habits with Established Ones: I connected monitoring my money with my morning coffee. This combination made the new behavior simpler to acquire.

4. Reward Progress: Small prizes for meeting financial goals may promote favorable behavior. When I paid off a major amount of my debt, I treated myself to a little celebration.

5. Responsibility: Sharing your financial objectives with a friend or family member may create a feeling of responsibility. I had a 'budget buddy,' a pal with whom I discussed my financial objectives and progress. This accountability helped me keep on target.

6. Reflection and Adjustment: Regularly reflect on your financial habits and be open to modifying your approach. If a specific tactic isn't working, don't be scared to try something different.

Through these approaches, I was able to alter my finances. I moved from being someone who lived paycheck to paycheck, burdened with debt, to someone with a growing savings account and a solid strategy for the future. It wasn't simple, but the peace of mind and financial stability I've acquired are well worth the effort.

This chapter focuses on recognizing and modifying damaging financial patterns, leveraging the power of consistency, and applying successful habit building approaches. This chapter balances practical advice with personal experiences, explaining how I successfully improved my financial habits. It intends to inspire and encourage readers towards developing their own sustainable financial habits, stressing patience, tenacity, and adaptation in the route to financial health.

Chapter 8: Investing in Your Future

Understanding Basic Investments

Investing is a crucial step towards financial stability and success. It might seem difficult, but grasping the fundamentals is vital for anybody trying to create money over time. Investments may be in numerous forms, such as stocks, bonds, mutual funds, or real estate, each having its own risk and return profile.

When I initially contemplated investing, I was overwhelmed by the choices and verbiage. To address this, I began educating myself through books, online courses, and financial blogs. I learnt that stocks represent ownership in a firm, bonds are basically loans to the government or companies, and mutual funds are pooled assets managed by specialists.

The main lesson here is to start with a clear grasp of various investment kinds and how they fit into your overall financial plan. It's not about jumping on the next fad; it's about making educated selections based on your goals and risk tolerance.

Making Smart Investment Choices

Smart investing selections are founded in research, preparation, and matching with your financial objectives. Here's what I learnt about making good investing decisions:

1. Diversification: Don't put all your eggs in one basket. Spreading investments across multiple assets helps lessen risk. For instance, I invested in a combination of stocks, bonds, and a little amount in a high-interest savings account.

2. Understand Your Risk Tolerance: Everyone has various degrees of comfort with risk. I discovered I was relatively risk-averse, so I picked assets that provided a balance between stability and growth.

3. Long-Term Perspective: Investing is not about becoming wealthy immediately. It's about expanding your money over time. I concentrated on long-term investments, avoiding the urge to respond to short-term market changes.

4. **Regular Investments**: I began investing little sums consistently, a method known as dollar-cost averaging, which helped me expand my investment portfolio gradually.

Risk Management: Learning from My Mistakes

Managing risk is a vital component of investing. I learnt this the hard way after a few errors early in my investing path. One such error was investing substantial money in a single company without appropriate research, attracted by the promise of great profits. When the stock's value collapsed, I faced considerable losses.

This incident showed me the necessity of risk management. Here are some tactics I adopted:

1. Research Before Investing: Don't invest solely on rumor or trends. Thorough investigation and comprehension of the investment are crucial.

2. Put Stop-Loss Orders: This feature enables you to put a sell order at a predefined price point to minimize possible losses.

3. Regular Portfolio Review: Periodically examining your assets helps you remain on top of performance and make changes as appropriate.

4. Emotional Discipline: One of the toughest components of investing is keeping emotions in control. I learnt not to panic during market downturns and to avoid hasty actions based on short-term market swings.

5. Seek Professional Counsel: As my portfolio increased, I sought counsel from financial professionals to make more educated choices.

Through these experiences and tactics, I not only recovered from my early losses but also established a broad and solid investing portfolio. The trip wasn't easy, but the lessons acquired have been crucial in crafting a more secure financial future.

This Chapter dives into the principles of investing, techniques for making sensible investment decisions, and the critical function of risk management, drawing upon my own experiences and blunders. The chapter tries to simplify the investing process for readers, giving practical insights and highlighting the significance of study, diversification, and emotional discipline in constructing a solid investment portfolio. It provides a guide for people wishing to take their initial steps in investing, demonstrating the long-term advantages of educated and planned financial planning.

Chapter 9: Maintaining Financial Discipline

Overcoming Temptations and Setbacks

Maintaining financial discipline is not simply about making rules; it's about adhering to them, even in the face of temptations and losses. It's a continual journey, loaded with trials that test your determination.

I've encountered my share of temptations — from the newest electronics to thrilling but unneeded trip bargains. Resisting these cravings wasn't always simple. Here's how I managed to overcome them:

1. Remind Yourself of Your Goals: Whenever I was tempted, I reminded myself of my long-term objectives, including becoming debt-free or saving for a home. This let me look beyond the immediate delight.

2. Avoid Triggers: I discovered my spending triggers and avoided them. For instance, if exploring online retailers led to impulsive buying, I curtailed my screen time on such sites.

3. Have a Support System: Talking to friends or family who understand and support your financial objectives may be immensely beneficial. They may give perspective and support when you're hesitating.

4. Plan for Setbacks: Financial setbacks arise - an unexpected payment or a sudden spend. What's essential is how you react. I developed an emergency fund to meet such emergencies without derailing my financial ambitions.

Long-term Financial Discipline: My Personal Strategies

Maintaining long-term financial discipline involves solutions that fit with your lifestyle and correspond with your objectives. Here are some ways that worked for me:

1. Automate Savings and Investments: I set up automatic payments to my savings and investment accounts. This 'out of sight, out of mind' strategy made saving straightforward.

2. Regular Financial Check-ins: I planned weekly and monthly check-ins to examine my budget, monitor my expenditures, and analyze my progress towards my objectives. This held me responsible and enabled me to change my goals as required.

3. Continuous Studying: I committed to studying more about personal finance. Understanding the world of money better qualified me to make educated choices and remain motivated.

4. Adapt and Evolve: My financial approach isn't fixed in stone. As my personal circumstances evolved, so did my financial plans. Flexibility and adaptation are crucial to long-term discipline.

Celebrating Financial Milestones

Recognizing and appreciating financial milestones is vital. It creates a feeling of success and pushes you to continue your financial path. Celebrations don't have to be costly; they should connect with your financial principles and aspirations.

When I paid off my first debt, I celebrated with a quiet supper with close friends. It was a tiny celebration, but it meant a lot to me. It was a crucial stride in my financial path and confirmed my dedication to my objectives.

Celebrating these milestones also serves as a reminder of how far you've gone. It's easy to forget the progress you've made when you're focused on the day-to-day. Taking a minute to reflect on and appreciate your successes can be immensely satisfying and inspirational.

This chapter covers the obstacles of keeping faithful to your financial plan, techniques for long-term discipline, and the benefits of celebrating financial accomplishments. Through personal experiences and practical counsel, the chapter covers frequent difficulties including temptations and disappointments, giving insights into how I managed to remain on course. It highlights the significance of frequent evaluation, modifying techniques to changing living situations, and acknowledging successes as a strategy to keep motivated and focused on financial objectives. This chapter acts as an inspiration and guidance for readers, illustrating that although the route to financial discipline is continual, it is both feasible and gratifying.

Chapter 10: Living Your Financial Dream

What Living Your Financial Dream Really Means

Living your financial dream goes beyond merely having a huge bank balance; it's about creating a condition of financial calm where money is a tool, not a cause of worry. It implies having the flexibility to make decisions that match with your beliefs and objectives, without the weight of financial restraints.

For me, fulfilling my financial goal meant being debt-free, having enough funds for emergencies, and being able to invest in my future. It also includes the less tangible but equally essential qualities like having the flexibility to follow my hobbies and the capacity to support my family without financial stress.

This dream could appear different for everyone. For some, it can mean touring the globe, for others, it might be about having a house or retiring early. The idea is to establish what it means for you and recognize that it's a dynamic aim, growing as you progress through various phases of life.

Real-Life Stories of Financial Success

In my path, I've met numerous amazing tales of financial achievement that have encouraged and led me. One such anecdote is of a friend who, despite a meager wage, managed to save enough to establish her own company. She achieved this by living frugally, planning properly, and prioritising her savings. Her tale showed me the strength of tenacity and the value of having defined financial objectives.

Another example is of a couple that successfully maneuvered their way out of serious debt. They consolidated their bills, formed a rigorous budget, and worked additional jobs to pay off their loans. Their story taught me the necessity of collaboration in financial planning and the influence of minor but consistent financial actions.

These anecdotes, coupled with my own experiences, highlight that financial success is not reserved for a privileged few with big earnings. It's feasible for everyone prepared to commit to a strategy, make educated judgments, and remain disciplined.

Preparing for the Future: My Final Thoughts

As I reflect on my path and look towards the future, there are many essential concepts I desire to share:

1. Continuous Learning and Adaptation: The world of personal finance is continually growing. Staying informed and being adaptive to change is key. Whether it's new investment possibilities or changes in the economy, being prepared to modify your approach is crucial to long-term financial success.

2. Building a Financial Legacy: It's not just about the wealth you accumulate, but also the financial knowledge and habits you pass on. I've realized the importance of educating my family about finances, ensuring they're equipped to make sound financial decisions.

3. Health and Wealth Connection: Taking care of your physical and mental health is as important as managing your finances. Stress, especially financial stress, can have a significant impact on your overall wellbeing. By achieving financial peace, I've also improved my quality of life.

4. Giving Back: Achieving financial freedom has allowed me to give back to my community. Whether it's via contributions or volunteering, being in a position to assist others has been one of the most fulfilling elements of my financial path.

5. The Adventure Continues: Finally, realizing your financial ideal isn't a final destination; it's a continuing adventure.

There will always be fresh objectives to pursue, obstacles to conquer, and lessons to learn.

This chapter describes what it actually means to fulfil your financial goal, sharing real-life success stories and delivering concluding comments on planning for the future. The chapter highlights that financial ambitions are personal and dynamic, stressing the need of constant learning, developing a financial legacy, keeping a balance between health and money, the pleasure of giving back, and realizing that the financial journey is an ever-evolving process. This concluding chapter tries to encourage and educate readers towards realizing their own financial aspirations, stressing the concept that financial freedom is not simply about money acquisition, but about living a life that is rich in more ways than one.

30-day Practical Action Plan

Here's a 30-day practical action plan designed to help readers curb impulsive spending and accelerate debt repayment. This plan combines habit formation, financial education, and actionable steps to create a solid foundation for better financial management.

Week 1: Assessment and Planning

Day 1: Financial Self-Assessment
Document all debts, income sources, monthly expenses, and any impulsive purchases from the last three months.

Day 2: Set Clear Financial Goals

Write down short-term and long-term financial goals (e.g., debt repayment, saving for a vacation).

Day 3: Understand Your Spending Triggers

Reflect on and note down what triggers your impulsive spending (emotions, environments, specific times, etc.).

Day 4: Create a Realistic Budget

Based on your assessment, create a budget that includes necessary expenses, debt payments, and savings.

Day 5: Plan for Impulse Triggers

Develop strategies to deal with identified spending triggers (e.g., avoiding certain stores, limiting online shopping).

Day 6: Unsubscribe and Unfollow

Unsubscribe from marketing emails and unfollow social media accounts that tempt you to spend impulsively.

Day 7: Reflection

Reflect on the first week. Note any challenges and adjust your plan accordingly.

Week 2: Building Better Habits

Day 8: Start a Spending Journal

Begin tracking every penny spent. This will make you more mindful of your spending habits.

Day 9: Implement the 24-Hour Rule

For non-essential purchases, wait 24 hours before buying. Often, the urge to buy will pass.

Day 10: Find Free Entertainment

Research and plan for free or low-cost entertainment options.

Day 11: Learn about Personal Finance
Spend time reading a personal finance book or article.

Day 12: Practice Gratitude
Write down things you're grateful for, focusing on non-material aspects of life.

Day 13: DIY Day
Engage in a do-it-yourself activity instead of buying something new.

Day 14: Weekly Review
Review your spending journal and budget. Adjust as needed.

Week 3: Debt Reduction Focus

Day 15: Prioritize Debts
List your debts in order of interest rate or balance (whichever repayment strategy you prefer).

Day 16: Create a Debt Repayment Plan
Based on your budget, allocate specific amounts for debt repayment.

Day 17: Cut Unnecessary Expenses
Identify areas in your budget to cut back on and apply these savings to your debts.

Day 18: Explore Additional Income Streams
Consider ways to generate extra income (e.g., freelancing, selling unused items).

Day 19: Negotiate Lower Interest Rates

Call creditors to negotiate lower interest rates on debts.

Day 20: Automate Finances

Set up automatic transfers for bill payments and debt repayments.

Day 21: Weekly Reflection

Evaluate your debt repayment plan and adjust if needed.

Week 4: Solidifying Financial Discipline

Day 22: Reward System

Create a reward system for meeting small financial goals (ensure rewards are not financially extravagant).

Day 23: Financial Buddy

Find a friend or family member who can be your accountability partner.

Day 24: Educate Yourself Further

Watch a documentary or listen to a podcast about personal finance.

Day 25: Review Financial Goals

Revisit your financial goals and assess your progress.

Day 26: Plan for Emergencies

-Start or review an emergency fund plan.

Day 27: Reflect on Purchases

For each purchase, ask yourself if it aligns with your financial goals.

Day 28: No-Spend Day
Challenge yourself to a day without spending money.

Day 29: Prepare for Next Month
Plan your budget and goals for the following month.

Day 30: Monthly Reflection and Celebration
Reflect on the progress made over the month and celebrate your successes (responsibly).

Continuation:

After the 30-day plan, continue to track spending, stick to your budget, meet with your financial buddy regularly, and adjust your plan as your financial situation changes. Consistency and commitment to these actions will lead to significant improvements in your financial habits over time.

Printed in Dunstable, United Kingdom